The
FASTIDIOUS
FELINE

How to Prevent and Treat
Litter Box Problems

Patricia B. McConnell, Ph.D.

Cover design by Julie Mueller of jam graphics
Photo ("Sushi sleeps") by Patricia McConnell

ISBN # 1-891767-04-6

For information, contact:
Dog's Best Friend, Ltd.
P.O. Box 447
Black Earth, WI 53515
608/767-2435

Printed in the United States of America

5 6 7 8 9

The
FASTIDIOUS FELINE
How to Prevent and Treat
Litter Box Problems

by Patricia B. McConnell, Ph.D.

Sometimes a person gets lucky. Very very lucky. They get a sweet, affiliative and cuddly cat who sleeps on their tummy, comes when called and never, ever goes to the bathroom outside of the litter box. Even if the box gets a little dirty. Even if the box is beside the food bowl and the washing machine.

And then, there's the rest of us. We get those other cats. Cats who would like to use the litter box, but don't like the litter. Cats who wish that the box was in a different location. Cats who are nervous about their environment and try to claim it with urine marks by the front door. Cats who leap up onto the bed and urinate on your pillow while looking right at you.

This booklet is for "the rest of us"—people who have normal cats who just might go to the bathroom somewhere besides the litter box. It's for owners whose cats haven't visited the litter box in oh-so-long. It's also for people who are getting a kitten and want to insure that their new cat is fastidious about using their box. So, if you have a new kitten, read the following section carefully to insure that your little cat gets off on the right paw. If you have a cat with an established behavior problem, don't just skip to the Treatment section. Many litter box problems are due to disagreements between you and your cat about what the bathroom should look like, so read the entire booklet carefully before deciding on your course of action.

1

DESIGNER BATHROOMS FOR CATS

There's no escaping the ultimate irony of cat ownership: cats are usually fastidious about where they go to the bathroom, which is one of the traits that makes them the perfect house pet. However, this same fussiness about their rest room often leads to problems—cats start going on rugs or pillows because something about the box just isn't quite right. You may think the box set up looks great, but hey, you're not using it, are you? Look at the box from your cat's point of view, not from your own.

The following section spells out what most cats seem to prefer. It's always useful to know the basics, so read through this section if you're starting off a new kitten or trying to treat a problem cat. While you're reading, remember that these are generalities, and none of us owns that generic beast "cats." We own individuals, who happen to be cats. In my experience, some of them have read the books and behave like we experts say they should, others make it up as they go.

TYPE OF BOX

Some cats couldn't care less what kind of box you provide, while others would rather die than go into that expensive, gorgeous box that you just bought. Here's what our generic cats like (or don't like):

Open boxes: Many cats prefer uncovered boxes, although there are plenty of cats who will put up with covers (including my cat, bless her heart). Perhaps some cats feel trapped inside a covered box, and avoid it because it seems unsafe. I'm sure that in some cases cats avoid covered boxes because the boxes get dirtier than if they were open. After all, the very covers that prevent us from seeing and smelling what's actually in the box make it easier to forget to clean the box. "Out of sight, out of mind" is not working to your advantage here, because your cat can't ignore the contents of his box. Since most of the odors are trapped inside, it can get pretty intense in there. If you are starting a kitten out I would use a standard open box to make going in the box easy and accessible. If you'd like to use a covered box eventually, try covering a second box, and switch to covered boxes exclusively once you're sure your kitten uses them consistently. If you have a litter box problem with an older cat I would be sure to have plain, open boxes available.

Clean Boxes: It's pretty simple, really. If you want your cat to be squeaky clean, why on earth would he go in a dirty box? I live in amazement of the number of cat owners who are furious that Fluffy defecates in their back bedroom, but provide nothing but a filthy box for their cat to go in. If you want your cat to be "clean" (as we define it) then you have to help your cat be clean. Think of it from your own perspective: What do you do when you encounter a dirty toilet in a public restroom? I turn around and walk out, and then try to find a clean toilet to use. And I don't have to put my paws in it, for heaven's sake. If you are raising a kitten or treating a problem cat, make a commitment to keep the box fastidiously clean. It really doesn't take a lot of time, the challenge seems to be getting yourself into the habit of cleaning it regularly and often. (A piece of chocolate every time you clean the box? Hummm, there are possibilities here!)

Clean as often as needed to keep the box fresh and attractive to your cat: scoop daily, or more often if necessary, and get on a regular program of disposing of "old" litter, even the "scoopable" kind. I can't tell you how often you need to clean the box, because it varies so much from cat to cat and house to house. Most people advise that you scoop daily and dispose of all the litter weekly. I have one sweet, amenable cat who is very laid-back about her box: I scoop every other day (she also goes outside) and refresh the entire box every week or so. If you have multiple cats or any problem at all, you undoubtedly will need to clean up more often.

Do be careful about using heavy-duty cleaning products to "clean" the box. Some of them actually help convert the urine to more ammonia, which is what creates that awful smell. Others of these products have smells that are aversive to cats, so simply empty out the old litter, scrub the box with baking soda and rinse, rinse, rinse. If the box smells of urine after all that then you probably need a new box. Ultimately, you need to be sure that the only smell left in the box is that of clean litter, not that of urine, soap, bleach or detergent.

No liners: Cats have been pretty clear about plastic liners that allow you to bag the litter and toss it away. They hate them. Convenient for you, but bad news for clean kitties. We don't know what it is about the plastic that so many cats dislike (non absorbent? bad smell? crinkly noise?), but hey, it's their bathroom, not ours! Don't start a kitten out with liners either, she may look for a better place to go and start a bad habit. Get rid of the liners if you have any litter box problems at all. Your cat adores them? Lucky you, just don't think this will mean that your second cat will.

Not too high: Some boxes are hard to get into and discourage cats from entering them at all. Most cats are great athletes; it's not that they can't jump in easily enough. The problem might be what they're jumping into. If they can't see into the box before they leap, they can't be sure what the landing pad might contain. Landing into a pile of yesterday's poop isn't conducive to litter box loyalty, so be sure that your cat can enter the box without a blind leap of faith. If necessary, construct a simple "step" up into the box so that your cat or kitten can check out what they're getting into before they enter.

The act of jumping in and out of the box might be a consideration for an injured or elderly cat. Some old cats who could easily jump into boxes when younger develop stiff and painful joints that prevent activity, and even young cats can develop sports injuries that make little leaps painful. Watch your cat and if you suspect any possibility that he is avoiding jumping into the box, then construct some steps and see if it helps.

If you have a cat who carefully enters the box, stands four square inside it with all paws in the litter and then somehow magically manages to drop urine or feces outside, take heart.

Those cats might do well with extra high sides (you can buy plastic storage containers that work great for these cats). Just be sure, again, to provide steps for the cat so that they don't have to leap blindly into their toilet.

Number of Boxes: There are a lot of reasons why you'd be very smart to provide your cat with more than one box. First of all, research on barn cats suggested that many cats preferred to urinate and defecate in different places. Secondly, I've seen a lot of clients' cats who stopped going outside of the box when we added another one, especially if the house is large or multi-storied. Having a bathroom on each floor is apparently important to cats as well as us humans. Some cats just don't seem to want to expend the energy to go all the way to the basement from the second floor, so they stop making the effort and start going in the guest room. Some cats get older and it hurts them to go up steps, so they resist trotting upstairs to the one box they've used for years when they were younger. Perhaps you have a second cat who has claimed the single box as their own and your first cat avoids the box to prevent a fight. Perhaps the location of the one box isn't just quite right, and the second box is in a better place, at least from your cat's perspective.

I'd use multiple boxes in several contexts: both to start out kittens (they really can't hold it for long when they're young, help them go in the right place any way you can!) or to treat or prevent a problem in an adult cat. If you have multiple cats this is especially important—multiple cats usually need multiple boxes. Read the section on location before deciding where to put the second or third box. The standard formula is "have one more box than you have cats." I've read it everywhere and can't for the life of me find where it came from, but I don't think we all need to follow this to the letter. I know many families with 4 cats and 3 boxes and no problems at all. But I do like the general suggestion to give your cat or cats lots of choices, and adding boxes has solved many a litter box problem in many a home, so don't be stingy with boxes.

It's important to place the boxes in very different locations. Three boxes side by side in the basement is functionally not that different from one big box, so be sure that your boxes are spread around the house.

TYPE OF LITTER

Effect of Experience: Cats learn at an early age what substrate (or material) is appropriate for elimination, and these early experiences have a profound effect on their behavior as adults. If you brought a 12 week kitten in from the out of doors, it may well prefer loose soil to litter at first. Some outdoor cats are happy to switch to soft sandy litter, but others are more set in their ways, so provide a box that has some litter on the side and what they are used to in the middle (see the Treatment Section for details). If you just got a kitten, start your young cat out on a litter that you can obtain often and easily, and then don't switch just because another type went on sale. If you have inherited a cat, make every effort to find out what substrate she has used in the past—if you can't ask, experiment with different litters in different boxes. She'll tell you what she prefers if you give her the chance. Worried you're catering too much to your cat? Not in this case. Remember the fastidious feline irony: if you want a fastidious cat, then expect her to be picky.

Sometimes a cat will have used one type of litter for years and then have an experience that results in an aversion to it. Perhaps the cat became ill and learned to associate the bad feeling of the illness with the litter. Eventually he went outside of the box on the carpet, just as he was recuperating. Voila! Now we have a learned association: "I feel better when I go on carpet, so that's what I'll do, and I'll avoid that awful sandy stuff that made me feel sick."

Generic Preferences: Our generic cats prefers soft, sandy litter, no added smells, and about one to one and a half inches of litter in the box. (This is based on the research of Dr. Peter Borchelt, a Certified Applied Animal Behaviorist in New York City, who gets a lot of credit in my book for being the first person I know to simply ask the cats!) My experience, and all the literature I could find, suggests that many cats are put off by scented litter (chlorophyll is one of the worst). What smells good to you might be disgusting to your cat (we are different after all—would you eat a mouse or lick your butt?) so don't buy something that smells extra "fresh and clean" to you. Your cat will probably hate it. And pay attention to the advice about not using too much litter. I violated this for years believing that a thicker layer of litter is somehow better. It's not, at least the cats don't seem to think so, and it's their bathroom. Perhaps they don't like the idea of their paws sinking into the unknown—who knows what's underneath? Whatever the reason, most cats prefer about an inch and a half of litter, so be sure that you're not using too much.

The only exception to this generic preference for sandy litter is if the cat has a paw injury. Fine sand can get into the wounds, so if your cat is recovering from a paw injury, try the pressed paper pellets called "Yesterdays News." Cats seem to like it much better than the shredded newspaper often recommended for recovery from paw injuries.

And do remember we're talking generic cats here. Every cat is different, and if your cat just adores the slaked lime type of litter and just won't switch to the scoopable kind, you can either try to switch gradually (either mix together or put the new stuff on the sides) or just give it up and honor the cat's original preference. What's critical is to let your cat tell you what he wants, and then accept it or try to change it gradually.

LOCATION

Take the Bathroom out of the Kitchen: Keep the box separated from your cat's eating and sleeping area. We humans like to keep those activities separate in our own lives, but don't intuitively generalize that to cats. I've had innumerable clients who had a "cat area," with the box, food and water all together in a little room. Some cats tolerate this, bless their hearts, but many put their paws down and simply won't go next to where they eat. I think these "picky" cats should get little ribbons for being so clean and neat, but some owners don't always see it that way. If you have a cat with a problem, or if you're raising a kitten, be sure to keep your litter and food areas separate. Why ask for trouble?

Quiet is Best: Choose a place away from daily traffic, entrances and exits, and appliances that make noise. Many a cat has been put off by a box sitting beside the furnace that kicks in just as Fluffy settles in to urinate. Refrigerators, furnaces, water heaters, dehumidifiers, etc.—all turn on and off by themselves and can be aversive to sound-sensitive cats. Don't put the box right beside them and end up with your cat getting afraid of the box.

Privacy: Most cats prefer to use the box in relative privacy. Many cats are put off by boxes that are in traffic patterns, by the front door, under a window or in the middle of a busy room. Go through your house and mentally record all the places that you might put a box that have some privacy. (Just to confuse things, some cats can profit by the placement of a box in not-so-private places, like right under a window-if they've been going there anyway, box or not. This is an exception that relates to scent marking problems. See the Treatment Section for more details.)

Safety and Escape Potential: The ideal box location is a private place that feels safe and has "escape potential." Some very private places that initially look as though they might be perfect don't actually provide what some cats want most: a quick way out. Cats want to know if someone or something is entering the room, and want somewhere to go quickly if they feel threatened. Sometimes just moving the box a foot or two in one direction is enough to get a cat to use the box again. I've had client's cats who stopped using the box in the bathroom until we moved it just 20 inches so that they could see the doorway as they were using the box. Apparently that was enough to make the box attractive again.

Escape potential appears to be the most important criteria to my cat, although no animal in my home has ever threatened her. She adores the dogs, who lick and kiss her, and there are no other cats in the house. But she grew up in the barn where she learned to be "on alert" all the time, so her favorite box is beside those very appliances that I told you to avoid. I think she likes it because she can leap up on the clothes dryer at a moment's notice. I'm just always careful never to start the dryer if she's about to use the box, and she seems to appreciate the ability to peer out of her box and then jump up and feel safe up on a high perch.

Easy access: Be sure that the boxes are easily accessible. Have at least one box per floor if you have a multi-storied house—lots of cats behave as though they get sick of having to go up and down stairs just to pee and so choose the guest room instead. Listen to the Realtors—a bathroom on each floor raises the value of your house to potential buyers—even, it turns out, if they are feline instead of human. Be sure that your cat doesn't have to go through a mine field to get to the box. If you have multiple cats, be aware that some cats guard spaces or boxes as their "territory," so be sure that one cat isn't preventing the other cat from access to the box (think carefully here, lots of clients have dismissed this as a possibility and then later discovered it was a serious problem).

The best approach is to walk around your house or apartment looking for a place that best fits the above criteria. You well might not have the "perfect place." Don't despair, your cat hasn't read this section. As I mentioned, my cat's favorite box is in the utility room, by the washer and dryer. It's covered, I don't always clean it every day and she uses it religiously. I worship her for it, and she knows it.

But when I brought her into my house I put many boxes on both floors, kept her food and water separate, and kept the box scrupulously clean. I watched to see which boxes she preferred, added a cover to one box while giving her access to two uncovered boxes. She chose the box I use now, the one with great "escape potential." That seemed to be the most important criteria to her, and that should be your guiding principle. Let your cat tell you what's important—if you want her to use it, then for heaven's sake make sure it is what she wants.

9

SUMMARY OF DESIGNER BATHROOMS
FOR FASTIDIOUS FELINES

- Use large, uncovered, clean boxes with no liners and sides low enough for your cat.

- Use sandy, scoopable litter with no special scents, about 1.5 inches thick.

- Have more than one box, and at least one on every floor.

- Put the boxes where there is privacy, safety and escape potential.

- Keep the boxes away from your cat's food, sleeping area and any noisy appliances.

- Keep the boxes as clean as you would like your cat to be!

SCENT MARKING

Some cats are perfectly happy with their boxes, but still choose to urinate or defecate on your best carpet or your new couch. The reason is probably based on the social system of house cats. House cats have evolved as territorial animals who exclude members of their own species that are not part of their immediate social group. Like many territorial animals, cats communicate to other cats by leaving urine and feces as "sign posts" —sort of like fences and "No Trespassing" signs in our own yards.

We really don't know exactly why some cats begin scent marking outside of the box, but our best guess is that these cats are trying to communicate to others about the boundaries of their territory. Perhaps, in some cases, cats want to surround themselves with a familiar scent. Since wild felines (and so many other territorial animals) commonly use urine and feces to maintain their territorial boundaries, it seems reasonable to speculate that this might explain that spot on your oriental carpet. Marking is most often performed by intact males, although it is also performed by unspayed females. Neutering male cats who spray urine is very successful: 90% of male cats who marked stopped spraying urine after neutering.

A stray cat showing up in the yard, tension between two (or more) cats in the same household, or even the disconcerting smell of a new couch can elicit scent marking. If your cat is spraying, or backing up to a vertical surface, raising his or her tail (yes, girls can do it too), paddling the front paws (a little like kneading, but while standing) and spraying urine straight backwards, then you can be sure that the motivating force is scent marking. However, don't assume puddles on the carpet are always about litter box problems: squatting and urinating outside the box can be motivated by medical problems, an aversion to the box OR a desire to scent mark different areas of the territory.

Sometimes we just can't tell exactly what is motivating a cat to go outside of her box, but often the location of the "accidents" can provide a lot of information. A cat who urinates just outside of the box, but right beside it, is often put off by the litter or the type of box, while the cat who consistently goes under an open window when other cats appear in the yard is probably scent marking. I'm just guessing, but I suspect that cats who urinate on their owner's beds, pillows or clothing are desperately trying to tell their owners that SOMETHING is wrong. My cat urinated on my pillow one night while looking directly into my eyes. After I came off the ceiling I went to clean it up—sure enough, there was blood in her urine. Poor Spices had been ill, and I hadn't known it. She deserves a lot of credit for figuring out a way to let me know! This was a medical problem, and is a good reminder to communicate any litter box problems to your veterinary clinic. One study showed that 15% of litter box problems were related to medical conditions. However, often the problem is related to what's been called "psycho social" marking—a kind of territorial angst in which the cat is anxious about maintaining his or her territory.

Is your cat "angry" at you? Lots of owners interpret their cats (or dogs) accidents in the house as spiteful, but anger at owners is a doubtful explanation for that urine spot on your carpet. More likely your cat is sick or stressed, so give her a break and try to help her rather than just getting mad at her.

TREATMENT

A word about punishment: Never punish your cat for going outside of the litter box. It's simply not effective, and can actually cause a lot of harm. I had one client who responded to finding an "accident" by grabbing his cat in a fury, thrusting him into the bathtub, and drenching him under running water. Needless to say, things hadn't improved much until he changed his approach!   There are some rare cases where a "remote" correction (a spritz of water or a thrown empty pop can) can be used along with the steps below, but those cases are few and far between.   If your cat is driving you crazy, don't feel badly about being angry, you are human, after all. Just don't take it out on your cat, it'll backfire on you.

STEP ONE: Be sure that your cat does not have a medical problem. Call your veterinary clinic and ask them the best way to proceed. Your veterinarian will probably want a urine sample to check for infection or crystals. Follow their instructions to obtain the sample, or bring your cat to the clinic and hand them your cat while explaining: "Here's the urine sample. I brought it in a handy, sterile package."   If your cat has a medical problem, you'll just waste your time trying the steps below if your cat has an illness that is not being treated, so be sure to be in communication with your veterinary clinic right away. Let me repeat the "right away" part! If your cat has been litter trained for years and "out of the blue" he starts going on the couch, get into action as soon as you can. I don't know about you, but my default is to live in hope for some period of time—taking the time honored "If I ignore this it will just go away" philosophy. I have to go out of my way to mobilize the energy to address the problem right away, so do what you have to do to take action. The longer a problem continues, the harder it can be to turn around.

One last comment about medical problems: I suspect that many cat box problems began as medical problems and then became learned responses to arbitrary associations. For example, your cat might have had an illness that caused painful urination, so that every time he urinated in the box it hurt him. He learned to associate the pain with the box, and begin urinating all over the house in an attempt to find a place where it didn't hurt anymore. Perhaps after he was diagnosed and treated he had begun going on the guest bed upstairs. Now he's learned that while it hurt to go in his old box in the bathroom, but it doesn't hurt to go on the bed, so of course he chooses the bed over the box. I suspect that this is a very common scenario, based on the number of cats that I see who are observed to go outside of their box, get treated for a medical problem but then continue to urinate in inappropriate places. If you think this describes your cat, provide him with alternate boxes and even alternate types of litter to lure him back into the box. I'd give him a tiny tasty treat every time I saw him leave the box, just to condition a more positive association with going inside the box.

Perhaps your cat had a medical condition that you and your vet successfully treated. After several weeks or months of good behavior, some cats will start going outside of the box again. If this is happening to you, your cat might be having a medical relapse. Several of the conditions that can cause problematic elimination can be tricky to treat, so don't assume that just because your cat had a clear urine sample last month that she's still 100%. Give your vet a chance to keep working with you, often it takes several visits to get your cat fully recovered.

STEP TWO: Consider neutering or spaying your cat, if he or she has not been already. Neutering a male cat who sprays is the single most effective method of changing the problem behavior. Although some neutered and spayed cats still spray, it is much less common than in intact animals. Intact male cats are famous for spraying, and it can be very difficult to

13

convince them to stop when their hormones are telling them otherwise. Don't set both you and your cat up for frustration, call your vet and make an appointment!

STEP THREE: Start a simple journal and write down when and where you find an "accident" (I just love that term, 'accident,' for a urine stain on the rug. It calls forth a vision of a cat saying "oh dear, I dropped my urine.") You don't need to make it fancy, but the more information you can gather about what is really happening, the more tools you'll have to help your cat. Don't trust your memory, it won't serve you well enough. You are looking for a pattern, both in where and when your cat goes out of the box and in changes in the frequency of the behavior. I spend over 45 minutes talking to clients about exactly what is going on, and often we discover that there is indeed a pattern to the cat's behavior that hadn't been clear before we took the time to talk it out. Writing notes, even very brief ones, can provide a tremendous amount of information that you well might need to solve the problem. Here's what you need to focus on for your records:

WHEN does it happen? Perhaps it's after you return home every night. (That happened to someone who worked with cats at a Humane Society. She now leaves her work shoes outside the house when she returns and all is well.) There might be no pattern at all, which still gives you information to use to analyze what's going on. Many people I talk to aren't sure when the cat actually went on the rug, they just find a urine stain "later." Be more proactive: if your cat isn't using the box, look as often as possible so that you can keep track of what's going on as best you can.

WHERE does it happen? Record exactly where your cat goes each time you find an accident, it's invaluable information. Is it the same place every time? Is it anywhere and everywhere? A lot of stains seem random at first, but after you start paying attention you might find a pattern: Always on wood? Always under the window? Beside entrances to the house? Right beside the box?

WHAT does it look like? Long thin urine stains caused by

spraying onto vertical surfaces are almost always scent marking, while round circles of urine on horizontal surfaces are usually from squatting. If the stain is on a vertical surface the cat is intentionally scent marking, while round puddles from a squatting posture could be either simple urination or scent marking. A long thin line on the carpet is usually from an animal who sprays urine without backing up to a vertical surface. Pay attention to the size of the spot: is it a tiny small spot or a huge round puddle? These are questions your veterinary clinic will ask you also, so pay attention to the details, they can be very helpful. (Frequent urination of small quantities of urine is a classic sign of medical trouble.) If your cat is defecating outside the box, then record if it is normal feces, soft or runny in consistency, or more smelly than usual. This can be a valuable clue. One of my client's cats began to defecate outside of the box after she switched to a premium brand of cat food. She (the human!) noticed that her cat's feces had a new and especially offensive odor from the new food. We switched the cat back to her usual food and presto! the problem was solved.

FREQUENCY is also important, and will be recorded automatically if you keep a simple journal and pay attention each day. You'd think you'd know if your cat is getting better, but it's actually tough sometimes when you're in the middle of the river to know if the flood is going down. Keep in mind that your perception of the problem may change— your cat may go out of the box five times a day for weeks, and after you start working on it, decrease the number of "accidents" to one every three or four days. If you've been dealing with this for weeks or months, you can get sensitized, such that just one accident is enough to upset you when it wouldn't have phased you two months ago. I bring this up because I see some clients who report back with discouraged voices that nothing has changed. When I ask about details they'll tell me that the problem now occurs at, say, five percent of the frequency that it did initially. Well, this is major progress. It's important to know if the treatment plan is helping or if it's not, but when you're sick of a problem a little bit can go a long way to discourage you. Try to separate your reactions to the problem from the facts of the problem. It'll help you to determine if you should stay with your plan or toss it out and start a new one.

STEP FOUR: Neutralize all areas where your cat has urinated or defecated out of the box. Cats are influenced by chemical signals when deciding where to go, and any area that has been used previously acts as an attractant for more use. After all, we all use some signal to tell us where to go— we humans use visual signals and look for the sign that says "rest room" and then for the round white thing. (At least I do—I'll skip the details of males vs. females. Thank heavens we don't need different boxes for different sexes in cats!) But while we use visual signals, cats use their nose If there's any smell of urine remaining in your carpet, it will trigger your cat to go there again. Be relentless in your search for urine odors! I get down on my hands and knees and crawl all over client's homes with my nose quite literally buried in their carpet. You'd be amazed at how much you can smell! If you can smell even a suggestion of urine, then your cat can't miss it.

Another effective way to search out urine stains is to use a black light. You can buy or rent them and turn them on in a dark room, pass them inches over the floor and look for telltale purple glows. Your vet can even give you a substance to feed your cat (Fluorescein) that will cause their urine to glow even more under a black light. It's especially helpful if you have several cats and don't know which one is creating the problem.

When cleaning up, don't confuse neutralizers with detergents. Detergents might get rid of the stain, but not the odor. As a matter of fact, detergents can set the odor into your rug or upholstery such that you have a terrible time getting it out. Neutralize first, then clean with detergent. There are many products available to neutralize urine odors, just be sure that the product is specially designed to neutralize urine. My favorites are "Nature's Miracle," "Outright" or "FON." Whatever you do, don't use detergent, bleach or vinegar. All three of those can make the problem worse, and that's the last thing you need. If you're stuck at home and can't get ahold of a commercial neutralizer, try mixing baking soda in water (try 1/2 cup to 1/2 gallon).

After soaking up as much urine as possible with paper towels, pour on the neutralizer so that the liquid comes in contact with every molecule of urine. Let it dry by itself, and then smell again. If it still smells, apply again. Old urine stains clean up better if you dilute them with water first before applying the neutralizer. If you have some especially tough urine-soaked areas in your carpet, try one of the liquid deodorizers mentioned above, let it dry completely and then sprinkle on A & H carpet deodorizer over night. Vacuum in the morning, and the smell just might be gone. I've had a lot of luck with this double whammy method for stubborn areas.

Any remaining smell of waste (especially urine) will stimulate your cat to continue to go in that area, so this is not the step to skip over lightly. There are some times where you have little choice but to bite the bullet and get rid of the offending carpet or furniture. This can be especially tough if you want to replace the furniture with something new, but are afraid that your cat will begin ruining the new piece. It's a vicious circle: if you continue with the old smelly rug or chair you are going to have a hard time changing your cat's behavior. On the other hand, how many owners want to risk expensive new furniture with a cat who is still going outside of the box? No one can tell you exactly what will happen, but if your cat has been going on an object that smells even faintly of urine you are going to have a heck of a time changing his habits until you remove the smell.

If you decide to bring in new furniture or a new carpet, you can physically prevent your cat from going to the bathroom on it for awhile. You have several different options, including keeping the cat out of the room unless you're there, or covering the chair with upside down plastic carpet runners (the kind with little teeth on the underside.) Most cats don't like stepping on a surface covered with little knobs, and the runners prevent a cat from performing that oh-so-satisfying pawing that they do when they're done urinating, as if to cover their waste. Many books recommend trying tin foil as a way to prevent urination, but my client's cats seem to think that tin foil is a great place to pee. Some cats will avoid the smell of citronella or citrus, while others will stay away from anything with a balloon on it, provided that you blew one up and popped it beside the cat after letting him sniff it first.

STEP FIVE: Give your cat every reason to use his or her boxes. Do everything you can to make the litter box perfect for your cat. Read the section on Designer Bathrooms and then survey your house. Ask yourself what the litter is like in the box, and whether you think your cat likes it. Compare it to what your cat is choosing to use outside of the box. For example, if your cat is going on a hard shiny floor, then provide a box with a hard shiny surface on the bottom and just a tiny bit of litter around the edges. Gradually you can add more litter once your cat is going back in the box. Let your cat tell you what he wants, and then replicate it in the box. If that helps, then gradually add litter, starting first around the edges of the box and slowly increasing the amount of surface area covered by litter. By the way, I've had several cats who preferred carpet, and I still admire their owners for the leap of faith it took to put carpet in the bottom on the cat boxes. After all, wouldn't you think carpet in the boxes would lead to going on any carpet in the house? Well, it could, but in these cases the cat was already going on carpet all over the house, so there was nothing to lose. This method did indeed switch several cats back to using their boxes exclusively, and leaving the carpet outside of the boxes alone.

Are there lots of easily accessible boxes? Do the boxes have privacy and escape potential? Are the boxes away from food, noisy appliances and sleeping areas? It never hurts to add more boxes and see if that solves the problem. Boxes are cheap, and once you get your cat in a box again, you can remove the ones that don't seem important. It can be discouraging to have multiple boxes around a little apartment, but it is so often effective it is universally recommended. (One client and I were so frustrated by his cat's behavior we considered hiring a dump truck to simply spread litter all over their home. Then we'd finally have a cat who only went in litter!). Getting your cat to use a box again is what it's all about, so buy some new boxes, and put them in new areas. Once your cat is using the boxes again exclusively you can start gradually decreasing the number of boxes.

Sometimes litter box aversions (or preferences for boxes that aren't available) are easy to spot. Your cat may shake his paws as he leaves the box (" yuck, I hate this stuff"), or avoid the box and go right beside it. Sometimes, however, it's harder to diagnose, especially if the aversion is related to the box's location. Perhaps your cat wants to be able to see the entrance to the room as he goes, and so has chosen several places around the house where he can accomplish that. This type of pattern is harder to find, but you can't lose by experimenting for a few weeks with more boxes, litter choices and different locations. Be clear in your mind that you are experimenting, and you won't get discouraged that the "treatment" didn't work. In an experiment anything that happens provides information. Say you buy three more boxes and your cat uses each one of them, no matter where they are and what type of litter they have. But she's still urinating in the living room. OK, granted this is not good, but at least now we know that it's NOT the boxes or the location, it's either medical or is a response to some territorial angst.

There's another way to make going in the box attractive, and I highly recommend it in most cases. You simply reinforce your cat for using the box. To do this effectively, you have to have organized an easily accessible treat, something that your cat really REALLY loves. Chopping up bite sized pieces of cooked turkey or chicken works well for most people. I just cook up a bunch (or buy turkey from the deli), cut it up in little pieces and then freeze it in bags of 10-15 pieces. One bag stays in the fridge, and I can easily go get a piece whenever I need it. Some of the commercial treats are great in that they don't have to be refrigerated, and you can just leave them in your pocket for whenever you need them. They tend to be full of sugar and/or preservatives, however, so be thoughtful about how many of them you want to give your cat. Whatever the treat, you are going to give your cat one as soon as she's used her box.

This is admittedly easier with some cats than others, since

some cats have predictable schedules while others seem magically to use the box only when you're asleep or out of the house. In some cases I've had clients pick their cats up and put them in the box and then give them a treat for using it, but please don't do this without discussing it with an expert—this can put many cats off and lead to more trouble. In most cases simply keep your ears pricked, and if you hear your cat using the box immediately give a verbal acknowledgment in a pleasant voice (don't yell!). Keep talking in a rolling, melodious voice and be there to give the treat when the cat starts to leave the box. The verbal praise is important, because I want your cat to know it's getting the goody for using the box, not leaving it, and your praise can act as a bridge to the treat. But don't sweat the small stuff here, this system can work even it it's pretty sloppy. If you only reward a third of the time your cat uses the box you may still get the results you want.

STEP SIX: Decide on a plan for "problem" areas. While you're doing everything that you can to encourage your cat to go in a box, simultaneously make it less inviting to go anywhere except in a box. You've already neutralized the problem areas if you followed Step 4, but you might have to do more than that if your cat is in the habit of going out of a box, say on the carpet in the study. Once you have old areas neutralized and new attractive boxes to use, there are three different methods you need to choose between to prevent the old habit from recurring.

One method that works in some cases is to chemically "re-mark" the area with smells inappropriate for bathrooms. Sometimes putting food and water bowls down prevents a recurrence of the problem. Sometimes spending time there yourself, sitting with a magazine and stroking your cat helps cats establish new habits. Perhaps covering the area with your and your cat's scent redefines the area for the cat as a bedroom rather than a place to eliminate. The idea here is to chemically label the area as an area in which any self-respecting cat wouldn't go to the bathroom, It has worked beautifully for some cats and their humans, and has had virtually no effect in other cases, so give it a try for a few weeks and see if it helps.

In one case, a cat began to urinate in her food bowl, which was not exactly what the owner and I had in mind. So we went to the second possibility: blocking access to the problem areas until the cat got out of the habit. We took up the food bowls and covered the offending area with upside down carpet runners, and provided new boxes in new locations. In this method you're not "re-marking" the area with different kinds of smells, you're just preventing an old habit from returning by mechanically blocking access to the area. Use upside down toothed carpet runners, bricks a few inches apart, or plastic to keep the cat away. If you try this, be sure that the area has been well neutralized. If not, as soon as you remove the barriers your cat will probably be back looking for his old toilet.

A third possibility is to put a box where the cat has been going. This is often very effective if the cat is going repeatedly in just one place in the house. It's a tough plan to adopt if your cat is going beside the couch in your living room, but remember that "job one" is to get the cat going in a box, any box. You can slowly move the box out of the living room into the laundry room if she starts using it instead of your rug, but you can't move your living room rug to the laundry room. If the living room provides her something that the other boxes don't, you'll still have problems related to a location preference, so be sure to analyze what she might get by urinating by the couch and try to replicate it elsewhere.

Choosing which method to use is as much an art as a science. Some problem areas save you the trouble of deciding: I've never asked a client to put a litter box on top of their couch, so if your cat is going on top of the furniture then you're pretty much restricted to mechanically denying access. The couch already smells like a resting area and sitting in used litter tends to put guests off, so this is a perfect case for carpet runners or plastic or better yet, closed doors.

STEP SEVEN: Eliminate the stress. If your cat is healthy but isn't using his box, Steps 1 through 5 well might take care of the problem. If, however, after you've tried everything above and your cat is still going outside the box, he might still be reacting to a "psycho-social stimulus" that is causing him to use urine (or much more rarely, feces) as a signal. In other words, he's marking areas of his territory in response to some external stimulus related to his social system or territory. As mentioned before, if he or she is spraying the walls, then you can be sure that the problem has something to do with his emotional state. If he's squatting on the carpet, then the problem could be related to the box OR some type of territorial anxiety. I suspect that box preferences and territorial marking are often related, and thus moving the box allows a cat to mark her territory in just the "right" place. If the problem is solved, the cause of it often doesn't seem too important.

It becomes important, however, if you've tried all of the above and your cat is still going outside of the box. Lack of success with experimenting with boxes is one symptom of territorial or psycho-social marking, as is urinating by the entrances to the house, urinating by windows or in response to seeing outside cats, urinating on new furniture, urinating out of the box when an unfamiliar human enters the house, or in response to social tension within a multi-cat household. (Cats don't have to fight to have tension between them, so don't discount this possibility just because your cats nap together in the afternoon sun.) This is always a challenging problem to diagnose and treat—there are so many things that could be influencing the cat that it becomes a kind of detective game to try to figure out what's going on in the first place.

Critters in your yard? If your cat is urinating beside or underneath windows, she might be responding to animals she sees in the yard. Some cats seem to be distressed by a variety of animals, and act as they are responding to squirrels, chipmunks, dogs and deer as territorial threats. I've had many clients who moved to a beautiful new house with picture windows overlooking the woods, only to find their previously perfect cat is peeing all over the white carpet. I suspect that these cats are intimidated by these gorgeous views that make humans so happy. In that case, we confined the cats to a few smaller rooms and let them adjust more slowly to the cavernous rooms and endless vistas out the window.

If there are outdoor cats harassing your indoor cat and he's clearly stressed about it, you need to find a way to manage the outdoor cats. Talk to their humans and request that they keep their cats inside, or at least in their own yard. Live trap them if they are stray cats (talk to someone with experience first), or build a fence. It's interesting that we humans think nothing of building a fence for our dogs but don't yet think of "cat fences" as a reasonable thing to do. Why on earth not? Oh yeah, there is that problem of money. If the expense of a fence puts you off, you might want to buy a motion detection system from an electronics store. They give off a heart stopping whistle if a small animal crosses their path (do warn your neighbors!). I've heard of a motion detector that actually sprays water on the animal instead of making a loud noise—sounds like the perfect cat deterrent to me!

Multi-cat household? If you have a multi-cat household, then adding more boxes and locations might have made a big difference already. Cats use different areas of the house differently, and one cat may be blocking access to either the room with the box or box itself. If moving boxes around hasn't helped and you think the problem might be related to tension between the cats, try conditioning the two of them to enjoy each other's company. Keep them separated when you're gone and only let them in the same room when you can actively work on conditioning the desired response. Start by giving one cat (let's call him Underfoot) a treat the microsecond he looks at your other cat. Every time Underfoot looks at cat number two (let's call him Midas), say "good" AS HE DOES IT and give him a tiny, tasty treat (it must be something he adores for this to work—turkey works well for most cats). Start with brief sessions in which Underfoot gets about 5 to 10 treats, and do this several times a day. After a few days, start putting the behavior "on cue," by saying "where's Midas" (presuming Midas is the other cat.) In a week or so, you'll be able to say "where's Midas," and your cat will look toward Midas and think "Turkey! Boy do I love turkey!" The intent here is to insure that Underfoot feels really good about Midas, because when he's looking at Midas, and therefore thinking about Midas, he gets something he loves. Eventually, Midas himself will become something your cat loves, just like I learned to love the awful shrieking buzzer in elementary school that meant recess had begun.

You can make this go faster if another person treats Midas at the same time for looking at Underfoot. If you're doing it alone and the second cat just walks over and starts begging for his share of the treats, no problem. Just feed them both, side by side, but continuing to say their name and treat them as they look at each other. This can help a lot if there is some mild tension between your cats, but if you have a clear problem about your two (or more) cats simply not getting along, be sure to contact someone with lots of experience in feline behavior and conditioning before working on it by yourself. I wouldn't mess with the brakes on my truck, because I just don't know enough to insure that I could do it safely. Believe me, your cat is a lot more complicated than my truck.

New family members. If you've found that the problem is related to new person in the house, have that person be the provider of the best treats in the world. If Underfoot is too afraid of newcomers to take treats from them, then you can do the same process I described above with a human, instead of another cat. The only difference is that once your cat becomes a little more comfortable with the new member of the household (because you've been giving him treats as he looks at this new human intruder), switch to having the new human toss the treats to Underfoot. Don't expect him to take treats from the hand at first; better to throw treats over to him if he's really scared.

Exercise. If any type of stress is related to your cat's behavior, you can't lose by increasing your cat's exercise. It's hard to say whether it's the exercise or the attention that helps the most, but some cats stop their inappropriate urinating when their owners schedule some concerted attention around a play session. Buy some new toys and schedule play sessions with your cat to get her moving around. Don't put them all down at once, I like to take a few up after three or four days and put others down for a few days; that way they always stay interesting. Some people teach their cats to wear a harness and sit outside with them, although I must warn you that going outside elicits indoor scent marking in some cats, so be cautious about this. And for all cats, there are some wonderful videos made just for cats of birds flitting around on the screen. I know cats who watch them for a half-hour at a time. Watching the cats watch the video is great entertainment in itself! Try this if you could use a laugh, which you probably do if your cat is peeing on your best leather chair.

STEP EIGHT: Confine your cat. A traditional recommendation for control of inappropriate elimination is to confine your cat for days (up to three weeks) to a small room. The room should contain little more than a box, food and water. The cat is denied access to other parts of the house, and then gradually allowed back into one room at a time. This can be effective in some cases, but only if all the steps above have already been taken. I have found this method effective in a few cases, but it's also aversive to both cat and owner, since most cats are happy to let you know how they feel about this change of circumstances, and talk to you about it non-stop. I've been using this method less and less, but it has helped in some cases.

STEP NINE: Aroma therapy for cats. (Not as crazy as it might sound!) If you've had no success with all of the above, you might want to talk to a Certified Applied Behaviorist or a Veterinarian about whether you should try using Feliway. Feliway is not a drug that you give to your cat, it is a spray that you use in areas that your cat has been marking with urine. It doesn't repel them, rather it is designed to replicate the scent marks from the cheek glands of a relaxed, mellow cat. We know from observational studies that cats perform facial rubbing at high levels when they are relaxed and in the presence of individuals that they enjoy. An enterprising French researcher deconstructed the chemical composition of the scent that cats deposit from their cheek glands and has created a safe, non-intrusive substance that appears to mellow out some cats. The hypothesis is that Feliway acts by surrounding your cat with the smell of relaxation and contentment, and acts to decrease their motivation to surround themselves with another scent. My first concern was whether cats would react as if another cat was in the house and mark even more, but I haven't heard of this happening. The smell doesn't seem to suggest another cat, it is so generic that it supposedly elicits the feelings associated with social harmony. This is a reasonable possibility, since we know that smell is a primal sense that is directly connected with our emotions.

It is of course not 100% effective (nothing works on every cat, believe me), and it can get a bit expensive. But so can destroyed couches and carpets, so if you've tried everything else I strongly suggest you give it a try. I've had a few clients whose cats simply stopped the problem behavior cold with the first application of Feliway and haven't regressed (yet, anyway!) I've also, predictably, had clients whose cats completed ignored it and continued their problem marking, yet their owners were out a nice chunk of change. Oh well, it was worth a try.

STEP TEN: Adjunctive medical intervention. Another possible course of action is to talk to your veterinarian about a medical intervention, and put your cat on an anti-anxiety drug. All drugs have side-effects, so you must only consider this unless your veterinarian is well aware of your cat's general health. The drugs that have been used successfully in recent years are 1) generalized anti-anxiety medications like Buspar (Buspirone), 2) Elavil (Amitriptyline,) a tricyclic anti-depressant and 3) Prozac (Fluoxetine). Each drug has pluses and minuses: Buspar has increased aggression between household cats in a small number of cases, while Amitriptyline can make some cats groggy and depressed. Prozac is new and expensive. Every case is different, but I think all cases share the fact that drugs should only be used after all other courses of action have been tried. If things are so bad that your cat's life is in danger, then I wouldn't hesitate to consider temporary medication, but don't look to drugs for a magic cure. If it is time to talk to your veterinarian about medications, help your vet by allowing him or her to do a full health check on your cat (including tests for liver function, for example) to be sure that the medications are safe.

And finally: Sometimes no matter what you do, you just can't get two cats to get along. I've had clients with multiple cats and no problems, until "that cat" comes along, and then everything goes to heck in a hand basket. Surely these intelligent, complicated highly social animals are similar to us humans, in that some individuals are like oil and water and simply hate each other from the word go. If you have a scent marking problem related to a multi-cat household, I encourage you to do everything you can to create a harmonious household. Be sure to contact someone who works professionally with cat behavior problems before giving up. But sometimes nothing seems to help, and the kindest, most loving course of action is to place one of your cats in another home.

This can be very difficult for cat-loving humans, especially those of us who want to rescue homeless cats and "fix" everything for them, and to whom placing them in another home feels like a failure. After years of working with behavior problems, I have come to learn that while I have accepted the responsibility of creating a loving, harmonious home for any animal I take in, my own home might not be the best place for any one particular individual. Don't make this decision alone, especially if you are attached to both of the cats. Often owners feel like "I've tried everything," when actually there are a number of things not yet attempted because the owner didn't know about them. So do go out of your way to contact a feline behavior expert before deciding to place one of your cats. But keep in mind (and in your heart) that it is not possible to fix everything for every animal in your own home. Rather, your job is to honor and respect the individual animal that you have taken responsibility for, even if that means placing him if a different home. I've seen many cats (and dogs too) who had a serious behavioral problem in one house which we never really understood and certainly couldn't cure, and later watched the same animal behave completely differently in another home. Perhaps it helps to remember how different each of us tends to be in different environments. We all contain many possibilities, and sometimes, whether feline or human, we need to change our environment to take on new personas.

TREATMENT PLAN SUMMARY

- Keep a journal and accurately observe and record your cat's behavior.

- Be sure that your cat does not have a medical problem; call your veterinary clinic right away.

- Consider having your cat neutered or spayed if you have a spraying problem.

- Neutralize the scent in all areas where your cat has inappropriately eliminated.

- Give your cat every reason to use his or her box: follow the steps above in the Designer Bathroom section.

- Prevent your cat from going on the "problem areas."

- Eliminate social stresses that might elicit territorial scent marking.

- If all else fails, consider Feliway or adjunctive medical therapy.